I0099484

ALL TIME HEROES

FROM ALL TIMES

~ Volume 5 ~

ALL TIME HEROES

FROM ALL TIMES

~ Volume 5 ~

THE LIFE OF
TAMAV KEREYA ISKANDAR

ST SHENOUDA'S MONASTERY
SYDNEY, AUSTRALIA
2016

All Time Heroes From All Times - Volume 5
TAMAV KEREYA ISKANDAR

COPYRIGHT © 2016
St. Shenouda Monastery

All rights reserved. Except for brief quotations in critical publications or reviews, no part of this book may be reproduced in any manner without prior written permission from the publisher.

ST SHENOUDA MONASTERY
8419 Putty Rd,
Putty, NSW, 2330
Sydney, Australia

www.stshenoudamonastery.org.au

ISBN 13: 978-0-9945710-1-4

Cover Design:
Hani Ghaly,
Begoury Graphics
begourygraphics@gmail.com

CONTENTS

Biography

"Now I saw a new heaven and a new earth, for the first heaven and the first earth had passed away, also there was no more sea…He who overcomes shall inherit all things, and I will be his God and he shall be my son". (Rev 21:1-7)

The above verse perfectly applies to our beloved Tamav Kereya who passed away from our foreign mundane world, rejoicing with Saint Paul saying, "I have fought the good fight, I have finished the race, and I have kept the faith. Finally, there is laid up for me the crown of righteousness…" (2 Tim 4:7-8).

She set eternity as her ultimate destination, choosing to live as a "foreigner" on this earth, leading a monastic life with all dedication and sincerity in her spiritual struggle, seizing every chance she had for her salvation through serving our

Lord and Saviour, and his children, with all the love and devotion one can ever feel or show. She chose to follow the wisdom that since one shall live only once, then one better do all the good they can possibly do, and render all the aid that is to the best of their ability without any sloth.

She managed to live by the verse that says "let us hear the conclusion of the matter: Fear God and keep his commandments, for this is man's all" (Ecc 12:13). She sought to acquire many virtues, worked hard, and indeed obtained many virtues, as we shall see later on in the book.

She truly lead the blessed life of the victorious martyrs and saints who kept the words of Christ and entered by the narrow gate, who were fortified by faith and managed to conquer all the worldly worries and tribulations by surrendering all to Christ without the slightest doubt nor uncertainty and proved, through their lives, that "for whatever is born of God overcomes the world" (1John 5:4).

May God assist us to tread the same blessed and righteous path of these saints, upholding virtues and faith with perseverance and hope, trusting Christ's word and promise "I have overcome the world" (John 16:33), "I am with you always, even to the end of the age" (Matt 28:20).

HER UPBRINGING

"I waited patiently for the lord; and he inclined to me and heard my cry, he also brought me up out of a horrible pit, out of the miry clay. And set my feet upon a rock, and established my steps. He has put a new song in my mouth-praise to our God, many will see it and fear, and will trust in the lord"(Ps 40:1-3)

Eugenie Iskandar was born in 1910, in a town called "Talkha" in the Dakahleya governorate, to righteous and wealthy parents who sent her to a Western Catholic School. She learned the French language until she became fluent in it. Her Father, Youssef, was a banker with a heart full of mercy and compassion. Generosity was his most eminent virtue. He used to give from his needs to the paupers and look after the needy; he would even sometimes have to borrow more in order to meet their needs. He didn't turn down anyone who would ask from him, just like the Lord commanded, "Give to everyone who asks of you" (Luke 6:30).

Eugenie grew up to take after him, as he had planted and watered this virtue in her ever since her early childhood. She would give everyone effusively with no discrimination and without much thought. She would put money in her purse, and on being asked, she would sink her hand in her bag, without even looking, and give whatever amount she had grabbed in her hand, and doing this she wouldn't let her left hand know what her right hand was doing. She also used to buy large pieces of material, give them to tailors to make clothing from it, and then she would distribute them to the poor.

However, in the days of her youth, she didn't have a strong relationship with God, nor was she well-attached to church, but she used to lead a worldly life, bearing much concern for trends of fashion, clothes, make-up, and all sorts of superficial matters. Furthermore, she used to encourage her friends to attend the movies with her, and would engage their thoughts with all these trivial issues.

HER CALLING

One summer, she was at a resort in Alexandria where she used to go, and there, God's grace was waiting to work and change her. When she first started to read the Bible, she felt so drawn to its life-giving words, and realised the vanity of her earthly interests. She then had a very strong desire to move from her path, to Christ's. So, upon that holy feeling, she immediately left Alexandria and returned to her own town with the decision that she would live with and for the Lord only for as long as she would live.

HER DISCIPLESHIP

She was introduced to the late Bishop Timothawos (Timothy), Metropolitan of Dakahleya, and became one of his disciples, and started to attend masses and meetings regularly at Archangel Michael's Church, in El Mansoura, growing spiritually and more and more in love with prayer. She used to pray fervently, waking up at any time of the night in her room to lift up her heart to the Lord, praising with David saying "As the deer pants for the water brooks, so pants my soul for You, O God." (Ps 42:1).

LEAVING FOR THE CONVENT

After a while, she felt that she needed to give much more

of herself to the Lord, so she seriously considered offering her whole life as a living sacrifice to God (Matt 19:29).

Before she became a nun, she used to take long retreats in her room in her father's house which she cleared up and laid out like a cell. But it was hard for her to continue peacefully due to various distractions, so she spoke to Bishop Timothawos about it and decided to move out to a convent.

The idea of monasticism ruled over her heart and mind, so she poured her thoughts out to her spiritual father Bishop Timothawos to whom, after seeing her solid will and persistence, it was then revealed to him in a vision that she was truly a chosen vessel for the Lord. He assigned her to the care of one of the monks who ordained her a nun, on Friday the 20th of June 1941, with the name "Kereya" (meaning "lady" in Greek).

When her father knew what had happened, he tried every possible means to talk her out of the idea of leaving. Nonetheless, she refused and insisted on continuing her austere life in the convent's surroundings (Luke 9:62).

On the 22nd of January 1944, she finally settled down in the convent of St Abu Sefein and was welcomed joyfully by the Abbess who told her that she was going to be a great blessing to the place.

LIFE INSIDE THE CONVENT

Tamav Kereya used to live with all humility, self-sacrifice and love for her sisters the nuns, taking upon herself a great deal of physical work joyfully and without a word of complaint. She used to attend to the sick and the aged among the nuns, apart from her regular kitchen duties as well as all sorts of cleaning tasks. Her motto was "I used to be arrogant in my father's house, but this place has taught me to do it all myself."

To humble herself even more, she used to commit herself to finishing the most despicable jobs that the rest of the nuns would try to evade like cleaning the convent toilets or the animal barn. That is how she gracefully gained the love and appreciation of the sisters who began to be drawn towards her. She won everyone's trust, to the extent that the blind Abbess asked her to be her daily Bible reader in her cell.

It was a divine arrangement that her cell happened to be adjacent to another nun's cell named mother Tawakleya, who shared the same virtue of generosity and hospitality. In that way, both cells became a blessed source of peace and comfort to all visitors who entered them.

She set St. Anthony and St. Shenouda as personal examples to follow, and used to regularly partake of Holy Communion, fasting and prayer at all times. She was humble, meek and forgiving in spite of any severe treatment she used to get.

Generally, she would spend most of the day labouring, and a great deal of the night rejoicing in intensive prayers and reading holy books. She was a great source of inspiration to her sisters, and because of that Satan envied her for the spiritual status that she reached in such a short time and tried to intimidate her in many ways. He once appeared to her in a vision in the shape of a huge terrifying serpent, and threatened her that he was always behind her and would never give up or leave her in peace. However, with all humility and steadfast faith, she overcame all his tricks and came out victorious against all the satanic warfare that was waged against her.

It is also worthy to mention that in 1947, she visited and took the blessing of the holy land in Jerusalem, the Church of the Resurrection, with the permission of the Abbess. She then stayed at the service of Father Mina, the ascetic (who later became Pope Kyrillos VI) who was also her confession father. He entrusted her with the service of preparing the wine for the liturgy, a service to which she was diligent.

Another credited detail of her life is that, she was one of the very few who managed to get the blessing of wearing the Holy Eskeem while she was still a nun at St Abu Sefein's convent, though it takes a great deal of patience and perseverance to follow its hard discipline. It was due to her serious and excessive abstinence that she deserved it. She used to perform up to 550 prostrations daily. In general, her life was full of virtues and merits as well as unceasing struggle till the day that Divine Providence chose her, and guided Pope Kyrillos VI into choosing her as the Abbess of Saint George's convent.

At first, she tried to escape the decision, as she felt unworthy of holding such a critical position. But God guided the Pope to appoint her as a Trustee of the convent first for a trial period of three months, during which the nuns felt her spiritual motherhood and so they rigidly held to her and refused to let her go. Finally, she consented to God's will and was officially ordained as the Abbess of St. George's convent on September 26th 1961, by the late Bishop Theophilos, the Abbot of the Syrian Monastery, along with Bishop Kyrillos, bishop of El Belina. She was the first Abbess ever to be ordained in the time of the ministry of Pope Kyrillos VI.

At the time she took up the yoke of service, the convent was lacking many facilities, so she prayed that God would provide for His place, and indeed, He did. She started renovating the cells with vast maintenance work and construction activities, including the convent's fortresses.

Also at that time, the nuns didn't have a church of their own to worship in, and had to go to a near-by church to attend the weekly mass. She therefore requested the construction of a small church on the ground floor, which was later turned into the convent library when another private church was built for the nuns.

She also built a small factory to keep the nuns busy and fill in their spare time. She later expanded its activities, by buying sewing, wool weaving, and embroidery machines. It had separate sections, some of which were for the making of priest, monk and deacon gowns, leather crosses, bags and other things.

Behind her was St. George who always encouraged the expansion of the Convent, and once he appeared to her and reassured her that he was keeping his eyes on the Convent, this was a great support and encouragement for her.

HER MOTHERHOOD

She used to watch over and follow up with every nun personally, encouraging and motivating them to adhere to the monastic rules, to persevere in their struggle, and persist in acquiring virtues, holding prayers, fasts and bible study meetings, contemplating on saints' biographies and their marvellous stories of spiritual struggle as a main source of inspiration. She emphasized punctuality in everything no matter how compelling the hindrances or distractions were.

The close relationship she had with the nuns began on her ordination and lasted till the day of her departure. During her early days as the Abbess in charge, and when the Pope asked her how the nuns were treating her, she told him that she wasn't living among nuns, but with angels. On occasions of feasts or celebrations, she went to every cell to congratulate the nuns individually, and if she did not find any of them, she used to wait for her till she came back.

Once a sister fell ill, and the pain intensified by nightfall, and Tamav had already tried to contact a doctor but couldn't reach him. So she stayed with her for hours trying to ease her pain with her comforting words, till she reached a point when she couldn't bear to see that sister suffering much longer. So she put on her uniform and went out to search for any nearby doctor. Fortunately, she ran into the priest of the convent with his deacon who managed to contact and fetch a doctor. She didn't go to her cell that night, till she saw that nun comfortable on her bed.

On her deathbed, in her sickness, the nuns attempted to try to take her mind off the pain, so they told her about another nun who was also ill. She was alarmed and didn't put the issue to rest till they got the other nun a physician.

On another occasion, one of the nuns started to suffer some symptoms that made her unable to see clearly and she gradually lost her eyesight, of course she couldn't read anymore. When Tamav learned of her condition, she dedicated a mass for her, put her name on the altar, and prayed faithfully for her. It wasn't long when, on the same day, the nun's sight improved and she was able to distinguish some words. This nun regained her full sight by the blessing of Tamav's prayers.

TAMAV KEREYA'S VIRTUES

MERCY

Tamav Kyrea was blessed with a life full of compassion and virtue, which are the pillars and the jewels of the true Christian monastic who is seeking God's way.

Amongst Tamav's numerous virtues, mercy and giving were the most prominent of them all, whether towards her nuns, the poor or the widow. She used to give to everyone without discrimination. She had compassion even over animals, where one of the nuns requested that they shouldn't give out much bread to lessen the amount of the left overs, to which Tamav answered that wild dogs and cats live off of these fragments.

She devoted Sundays and Fridays of every week to host and feed the poor. She never scrutinised how much she used to give. Once she was asked so many times by the same woman for money, and though many nuns grumbled and criticised her for that, she didn't turn her down, not once. She also used to carry around change in her pockets in case she was asked by anyone.

One day some poor children stopped her and begged her for some change, but she had already run out. Suddenly a lady came running towards her, reached into her purse and then handed Tamav a sum of money. On examining the money, she found it all in change! She asked the lady why she would give it all in five and ten piaster coins, she told her that St. George appeared to her in a dream and reminded her of the money she had promised to give to the poor, and also requested that she would give it all in these coins. On hearing that, Tamav rejoiced and praised the Lord and his saint who knows exactly the needs of his children.

On another occasion, a pauper knocked on the convent door for money, so she asked a nun with her to reach into her pocket and give him whatever comes out in her hands. The nun did so, and found two pounds (equivalent to $22 today). She thought it was too much, but Tamav insisted on giving him the whole amount.

She loved children so much, she made a charity box for them so that whenever they came, there would always be coins to give them. They used to come to her and take what they needed from the box. Some of them used to come to her more than once a day, the rest of the nuns wanted to rebuke them, but she used to remind them of the Lord's words "Let the little children come to me, and do not forbid them, for of such is the kingdom of heaven" (Matt 19:14).

On another day, a salesperson selling brooms was wandering around the convent, so she stopped him to buy a broom. She asked him about the price, and he said it was for three piasters. She objected to the price, so he persisted that he couldn't cut the price down as he thought she was trying to bargain, however; she said to him that three piasters were nothing those days and that she thinks that the broom was worth more, and that she was willing to pay five instead. The man was amazed when he took the money, and wished her well. When the nuns questioned her about what she did, she told them it was the best way to help him out without injuring his pride.

She used to financially aid many families secretly. It

happened that one of these families stopped coming to get help for over three consecutive months, so she became worried that something might have happened to them. She asked the brother of one of the nuns to go check up on that family. While she was talking to him, he found her hurrying down the stairs to meet a lady from that family he was about to check up on and so they all wondered at how fast God had responded to her prayer.

Something similar happened three days before her departure from this world, where she appeared very anxious as she was treading back and forth between the main convent gate and the waiting room, as if she was expecting an important person. This was because an old pauper did not come as usual to collect his monthly assistance, and she did not settle down until he had arrived and had received the envelope.

Tamav Kereya constantly offered meals to the brothers of the Lord as St Abraam, the late Bishop of El Fayoum used to do. This encouraged the expansion of the service, so that Tamav Kereya built a dedicated hall in the garden at the entrance of the convent and appointed a nun to attend to the needs of the brothers of the Lord. This hall is still being used to this day for this service.

It is not accidental, but a heavenly order that Tamav Kereya's departure coincided with one of the meetings of the brothers of the Lord at the nearby church of St George, resulting in a huge number of people weeping and crying while walking in her procession.

Tamav Kereya was once described by one of the Fathers as St Abraam the Second.

GENEROSITY AND HOSPITALITY

Tamav possessed a heart full of love for everybody without any discrimination; to the point where every one loved her so much they used to call her "Ya Ummy", that is, my mother. She often quietly took part in solving individual family problems, either alone or with other priests, and with the blessing of God was successful.

HUMILITY AND SIMPLICITY

These virtues were so evident in mother Kereya that everything about her such as her demeanor, appearance, clothing and cell were all very simple.

Even though she used to humble herself before everyone, God would always lift her up. All loved her because whoever would come across her would never feel that they were dealing with the head of the convent but they always thought she was an ordinary nun.

Once a government official rang the convent and asked to speak to the responsible mother, and it happened that she had answered the phone herself. When he asked her who she was she answered, "I am the servant of the convent".

Even when she used to receive important visitors, she wouldn't change her clothes or dress up in a way to project herself as the Abbess of the convent. She would meet everyone as she was. When she was asked why she didn't change and dress up accordingly, she would answer "This is how I am going to stand before God, so why would I be ashamed of it?"

Also out of simplicity, she would pay just as much attention to any little child as she would to an adult, offering children candy and chocolate to cheer them up.

She used to joyfully accept peasants' offerings of vegetation and fruit and would never look down upon any of them no matter how little the gift was. On one occasion, a peasant girl brought a small chick to her and she took it with so much joy just like Jesus accepted the little offering of the widow.

Her cell was so humble and simply furnished, bearing no signs of luxury. She was austere in everything including food.

She had a very pure heart that would never take offence at anything and would never hold grudges. If any nun offended or disobeyed her, when they would come back to apologise, with a forgiving smile she would just say "What for?" and would then kiss her hands. It was her humility that attracted visitors to the convent for comfort and edification.

LIFE OF PRAYER

Tamav Kereya had such a deep great passion for prayer that she used to say that praying is the best way to be united with the Lord. That is why she used to pray fervently and unceasingly at all times with such passion and awe. It was her only source of consolation. She prayed for everyone, on all occasions, good or bad alike and every time the convent would be suffering a certain problem, she would just go to the icon of St George and plead with him to interfere and resolve it. At other times, she would put the problems on the altar, very certain that she had placed them at the feet of Christ Himself.

She led a life of prayer. During St George's feasts, she would withdraw herself from the crowds politely, and resort to her cell to keep her prayer times, as God was the only close person to her. She was so strict in keeping constant prayers that she couldn't bear a day to pass without lifting her heart to God in prayer. She used to ask one thing from the Lord which is, that he would take her soul after she fulfills her prayers, and so it happened that she passed away on the day when she fell gravely sick and couldn't stand up for prayer.

She was diligent in her prayer and so would start her day at 2AM with the midnight prayer and then Tasbeha. She often felt the presence of the spirits of the saints praying with her. She used to be totally absorbed when praying that anyone who saw her would be blown away by the sight of her. She would then go down to where St George's relics were kept to have her daily chat with him. To show his love for her, he would move the chains so he would make his presence felt to her in a physical communicative sense.

She was also regular in attending masses, and would never miss one on any day. She would stand still throughout the mass, even as she was getting older, as she used to derive her power and strength from it.

PROPHECY

God only reveals His intentions and will to those who are pure in heart and mind. He entrusts only the humble with His gifts. Tamav Kereya used to live in the spirit and thus deserved all divine talents.

A visitor was bringing an animal to the convent as he had made a promise to St George, and on the way he ran into an officer who stopped him and questioned the sacrificing method he was about to use with the animal. The officer became very rude towards him and punched the man many times in the face. He was about to confiscate the animal off of the visitor, who then started to call upon St George to save him from the altercation. The officer tripped over and fell on the ground. He felt it was a bad omen, and got up and let the man go his way.

When the man reached the convent, Tamav received him

with great hospitality and brought him refreshments and asked the sisters to let him rest "as he has gone through great trouble just to bring us the sheep". The man was amazed by her words, as he had not yet told her about what happened to him on the way.

Another lover of St George was visiting the convent and tells that he had a little amount of money, not sufficient to buy a new car which he really needed. One day he turned up to the convent and with a doubting tone, he asked Tamav "Can St George really help me find a new car at that price?" With certainty, she answered him "Don't worry, you will get a new car at that price."

The man left after he got her blessing, and on his way, he came across a butcher's shop in front of which a brand new car, the latest model, was parked and had a sign "For sale" on it. The man went to inquire about the price, and was surprised to hear from the butcher that the price he was asking for was the exact amount that he had. The man got the car and glorified God and thanked Tamav.

Another encounter took place with the exact same man just two days before Tamav's departure to heaven. She called him up and asked him to bring his wife and little daughter to the convent for them to see her. When they all got there, they heard her saying to them "That is it, I am about to leave". Of course they didn't understand what she meant by that as she kept on repeating it many times. When he asked her what she meant by that, she told him "Tomorrow you will hear and understand". After she passed away, he heard the news on the same day and only then he understood and cried bitterly.

Also Father Angelos El Soriani used to minister the holy mass for the nuns every Tuesday. But due to sudden obligations, he couldn't come to the convent for quite some time, till only one day before her departure, she asked the sisters to open the door to receive Father Angelos, even though he hadn't informed her that he was coming. When the nuns opened the gates, they found him about to knock on the doors and were all amazed and glorified God.

A monk mentioned that when he was young, his mother used to take him to the convent to see Tamav and get the blessings of the place. He mentioned how he was always the subject of his mother's constant complaints because of his improper behaviour. He also said that on one occasion, Tamav reassured his mother saying that someday he will make a very good monk. His mother found it too hard to believe but, from then on, he kept on visiting the convent by himself and on every visit, Tamav would ask the sisters to prepare some food for their "future father" prophesying his becoming a monk. And so it happened!

There was also a couple that were having great difficulties having children. One day they were at the convent and asked Tamav to pray for that problem that God may grant them offspring. She prayed for them and reassured them that "Around this time next year, you will come back with a little George in your arms." And so it happened that God gave them a baby boy whom they called George. Later on, they had five more children.

Also a medical student was very worried about her exam results and asked Tamav to pray for her. Tamav assured her that she would get a "credit" grade overall. When the results came out, the girl found fulfilment of Tamav's words as she got that exact grade.

She also prophesied about one of the nuns' fathers becoming a priest, and shortly after, they heard the news of his ordination. Also she had the same prophecy about another servant that she saw in a vision as a fruitful tree and even gave him the name of Father Mikhail. And shortly after she passed away, that servant was ordained as a priest by the name of Father Mikhail.

One day, Pope Kyrillos gave Tamav a wool string to weave into a jumper. In turn, Tamav assigned it to one of the nuns to make the jumper out of it. However, another priest asked the same nun to make him a pair of woollen socks, knowing that she is good at weaving. The nun thought to herself that she should finish the socks first since it is a small job that would take only a matter of days and then she can start on the jumper for the Pope. Tamav asked her to finish the jumper off, as she won't need to do the socks. Two days later, the priest passed away!

Another lady told a story that that she attempted her commerce diploma exams twice and failed for two consecutive years. Her family used to reproach her harshly and give her hard times over it. She fell into despair and decided not to attempt the exams the next year and gave up on her studies. She went and told Tamav about her problem, who encouraged her to continue till the end of the path and assured her that she was going to pass.

On the day of the exam, the lady attended a mass with Tamav in the convent just before the examination began. During the mass, she saw a nun kneeling down all through the mass, and by the end of it, she was no longer there. When she asked Tamav Kereya who that nun was, she told her that she was a previous nun who passed away years ago, but she is used to attending the mass with them in spirit. The lady was stunned and glorified God, and went on her way to the exam with such overwhelming feeling of peace and comfort.

She sat all her exams, and when the results came out, she went straight to the convent to get the blessings of Tamav Kereya who was waiting by the gates of the convent to receive her. She congratulated her on passing, even though she hadn't heard the results yet. When the lady went to check the results, she found out that she had indeed passed!

Even after she got her first job, she was extremely uncomfortable with her boss' treatment of her, and she had often complained to Tamav about him. She once told her that she was going to get a new job, a promotion, even though she didn't have the expertise for it. A few days later, all that Tamav had said came true and she was the one chosen for the position, and she was very happy with it and glorified God.

Before her departure into heaven, she had told a very respectable lady, a regular visitor of the convent, that "it is drawing near now, I am going to go, and one of the daughters of Tamav Ereni, the abbess of St Abu Sefein's convent, is coming to take over here, receive her well". That was only one week before she passed away.

Once, Tamav was visiting St Abu Sefein's convent and was sitting by the gates when she saw Mother Yoana closing the gates. Tamav told her, "Give me the keys and don't worry about the gates as long as you take care of St George's convent on my behalf." Mother Yoana was shocked but thought that Tamav Kereya was just joking. However, that was a prophecy telling her that she will take charge over the convent after her departure, and that is truly what happened.

Another lady mentioned that during the celebration of the feast of the arrival of St George's relics to the convent in July 1980, she heard Tamav Kereya requesting from three different people to prepare enough food for all the visitors as she wants everybody to eat and not go home hungry as it is her "last feast with them this year". And indeed it happened that she passed away the month after, August 1980.

Also it happened that another nun fell gravely sick before Tamav's departure. As that sister was passing through the most dangerous state of the illness, everybody who was looking after her expected her death at any moment. But

Tamav assured them that it will happen with her first, that she will go before her, and indeed she departed first.

Tamav's relationship with the saints

SAINT GEORGE THE PRINCE OF MARTYS

She greatly loved him, as he was her personal patron saint. She had always resorted to him whenever she had to shoulder many problems or when the affairs of the convent would get complicated. Whenever she asked for his interference, he would step in and resolve all the issues. She used to approach his icon or his relics and would knock on it as if she was calling upon him.

Once they needed to buy some provisions and other requirements for the convent and Tamav asked one of the servants to go and buy them for her. When he gave her the total sum, she discovered that there was not enough money in the convent to pay him and was so embarrassed. The servant offered to pay for them, but she asked him to wait till she tells

St George. She came back with a smile and assured him that "St George will take care of it and the money should be on its way any minute!" Five minutes later, a man came to visit the convent, with an envelop in his hand containing the exact amount of money needed as a donation!

Another man tells his story:

Once I was on a visit to the convent and I stayed for a couple of days. During my stay I fell very sick and was very tired. My temperature was fluctuating from 36-40oC and I had a severe case of vomiting and diarrhoea. We tried to find any nearby doctors, but unfortunately no one was available as it was during Ramadan and everyone was unavailable, especially as it was close to their breakfast time.

Tamav was very concerned about me, especially after I left with two other friends of mine who supported me on their shoulders. On our way out, we suddenly came across a cab that stopped right in front of us and the driver invited us inside, saying that he was going our way.

On the way, he told us how he had been stopped by a high-ranking officer with many medals on his chest, telling him that he was going to meet us and that he must offer us a lift home, informing him that one of us is really sick.

After I got home, I was severely ill. I got checked by a doctor, who was not optimistic about my state and told them, "He would be lucky if he lives to see the morning." He gave me some medication and fluids, as I was gravely dehydrated.

Around midnight, I woke up suddenly to find St George on his horse, as typically depicted in icons, standing beside my bed. I was so amazed and baffled, I even asked him "Is that really you? Here in my room?" He smiled and said, "Yes, Tamav was so worried about you that she asked me to come and check up on you." Then he did the sign of the cross on me and said "You are alright now, just get some rest" and then he disappeared.

I woke up the next morning so refreshed and energised with no signs of weakness or tiredness any more, and all the symptoms had disappeared. I went back to the convent to praise God and reassure Tamav Kereya and let her know that I had recovered.

Another man tells his story:

I used to suffer from a hernia for so many years that it became intolerable. Tamav encouraged me to get an operation done, but I was reluctant and scared. I acted upon her advice and underwent the operation. For five-days after the operation, I suffered from a high temperature and felt that my body was slowly disintegrating, and then I went into a coma for several days.

During the coma I dreamt that I had seen St George with a nun on his right-hand side and he anointed me with holy oil. I remember having a conversation with him and the nun. I woke up from the coma the next day all sweaty, a healthy sign that the fever was gone, and my roommate in the ward who was a Muslim, asked me who St George is. I was surprised and I asked him why? And he said that he heard me talking to him all night long.

Suddenly the phone rang. I picked it up to find Tamav Kereya on the other side asking me "has St George come to you yet? I sent him last night." I told her about my dream and how much better I felt then and I went back to the convent shortly after to thank him and praise the Lord.

Another man tells a story about one of the workers who used to do maintenance work in the convent, who was a non-Christian. That man was a bit of a fanatic, he had always strictly refused to socialise with the other workers or even eat from the food the nuns used to serve to the workers.

One day he was installing the church bell up the tower when he slipped and fell from the tower and broke a lot of bones. He almost died and was in a very critical state and was immediately carried to the hospital. There the doctor ran some tests and x-rays to decide whether or not to go ahead and operate instantly to save his life. At night, before they decided on the operation, the man tells that he saw in his sleep, a very handsome doctor with a very bright face approaching him saying, "why don't you like the nuns and why don't you ever eat of their food? If I were you I would apologise and have whatever they offer me." Then that doctor touched my legs and said "there, you are alright now, go to the convent first thing in the morning and apologise." The man woke up in the morning to find the doctors around his bed amazed that they found nothing wrong with him anymore.

He praised God and went to the convent and apologised warmly to Tamav Kereya and finished all his work and even participated in other works and when done, refused to charge them any fees for his labour.

Another story:

One day, a great number fish fillets were given to the convent. They needed a lot of oil to fry it in order to feed the multitude of visitors, but because of an economic crisis, the oil prices increased sharply and the convent couldn't afford to buy enough oil to cook all the fish, and at the same time, the fridges in the convent couldn't accommodate the fish either. This situation really caused great distress to the nuns. Just like every time, Tamav went down to the icon of St George and knocked on it 3 times and asked him passionately to get them out of this predicament and provide oil for the convent.

A few minutes later, she saw a lady with flour and paste traces on her gown, as if she had been kneading, rushing hastily towards her and offering her oil. Tamav wondered what her story was, and the lady said "I was home baking some bread when I suddenly got this overwhelming feeling that I should leave immediately to the convent and pay off what I had promised St George which is this amount of oil. I tried to resist that desire till I finished what I was doing, but somehow I felt compelled to come at this moment and do as I promised." The nuns were greatly relieved and amazed at the way St George caters for the needs of his convent and how close Tamav Kereya was to him.

Later on the same day, another lady called the convent with 20 kilograms of oil saying that her son in America had called her all of a sudden to urge her to get the oil and take it to the convent without delay.

Another child was suffering a chronic case of asthma that some times led to serious suffocation. Her parents, with a great deal of faith, brought her to Tamav Kereya to pray on her so that the asthma attack would leave her. Tamav was deeply moved by the state of the child and carried her in her arms and went down to the icon of St George and stayed there praying so fervently and begging for the child to be healed. The child started to recover during Tamav's prayer, who didn't stop praying till the child was completely healed.

HER RELATIONSHIP WITH ST POPE KYRILLOS VI

The relationship between Tamav Kereya and St Pope Kyrillos VI dates back to the days when she was still a novice nun at St Abu Sefein's convent, as she was learning at his hands when he was the priest Father Mina. She had always served him, even after he was ordained a patriarch, tending to his service clothes and his personal needs till he passed away.

On Tuesday, the 9th of March 1971, the Pope called her up and asked to see her and the nuns urgently, as he was accustomed to seeing them every Saturday of the week. When they had all gone to visit him, he bid them farewell saying, "My children, I am going away very soon and I need you to take care of yourselves and pray for me." Tamav was surprised, as he didn't request that she prepare his luggage and travel needs as he usually did. When she asked him about what he needed, he said to her "it is alright, I am going to a place where no luggage is needed." As she wanted to have his signature for an approval document of nine novices to be ordained nuns, she had to give him the paper to sign before he left, and so he did.

Two months later, on the 14th of June 1971, she received a phone call from Mr Wadei informing her of the news of the Pope's departure to heaven. She was struck by the news and grieved in her soul as she finally got the message he was trying to convey to them when he asked to meet up with them previously the other day.

The relationship between them didn't come to an end; on the contrary, he became one of her patron saints together with St George.

<u>One of the servants tells this story:</u>

I used to serve another convent, other than St George's, and was very close to that place. I only used to visit St George's from time to time, as I wasn't nearby regularly. Once I had a big fallout with another servant in the other convent who really insulted me and my service, and I stopped going there ever since. One day I was at home half-awake, when I saw Pope Kyrillos VI standing before me and talking to me saying, "don't be upset at that person, get up and pay St George's convent a visit and pray there as Tamav Kereya needs your help." I was astonished and went to St George's the next day to find Tamav Kereya standing by the gates, as if awaiting my arrival. She welcomed me warmly and asked me to do a couple of things for her. Then I started to become a regular there. One day I got a phone call from the person who offended me in the other convent asking me to come back, however, I politely apologised and told him that I forgave him already but can't go back as Tamav needed me around that time of the year.

<u>The same servant tells another story:</u>

I once had an issue that was concerning me much and I was praying a lot for guidance in that regard, asking for the advice of Pope Kyrillos in particular. I prayed a lot one night and then went to sleep. In the morning I headed to the convent to pray the mass there. I met with Tamav Kereya after the mass to find her surprising me saying, "Did Pope Kyrillos come to you last night?" I said, "Yes!" And we spoke about that issue, and she said, "I know, we always do Tasbeha together every night and he told me that he spoke to you." Then she paused all of a sudden and looked regretful for saying what she had said, as if she revealed a secret, and she asked, "What did I just tell you?" Then she withdrew to her cell and everybody could hear her weeping, rebuking and disciplining herself with many prostrations and praying. That is because she didn't want to brag about her close friendship with the saints.

APPARITION ON THE FEAST OF PENTECOST

In the year 1980, the year of her departure, she was praying on the day of Pentecost in the convent, when people saw her moving suddenly towards the altar of St George and kneeling, then standing up about three times, then leaning her head forward. She then moved back to her place. After the prayer, one of the nuns asked her about her strange movements during the prayer.

Tamav: "Didn't you see him?"

The nun: "See who?"

Tamav: "Pope Kyrillos!"

The nun: "No!"

Tamav: "He was right there, standing by the altar doing the sign of the cross at me and blessing all the nuns around!"

TAMAV'S DEPARTURE

A few days before her departure, and after a long exhausting day of meeting visitors and convent labour, she retired to bed early to get some rest. In a vision, she dreamt as if she was taken in the spirit to a very beautiful place where a very handsome man with a luminous face was waiting for her. When she drew closer, she recognised him as St George. He took her on a tour and suddenly came to a stop in front of an empty elegant and beaming seat. When she wondered whose it was, St George answered her "It is yours!" Out of humility, she felt unworthy of it and said "But what have I done to deserve this place?" He answered her "All the deeds of mercy and charity have qualified you for this place."

TAKE HER BLESSSING BEFORE HER DEPARTURE

One day, a priest from a governorate in the Delta, Lower Egypt, called the convent to visit it for the first time. When the nun responsible for the gates opened to him, the following conversation took place:

Priest: "Is this St George's convent?"

Nun: "Yes."

Priest: "Is the Abbess of this convent called mother Kereya?"

Nun: "Yes, why? Why all these questions?"

Priest: "Pardon me, I have never been here before, but last night, I was visited by St George in a dream telling me to come and attend the mass this weekend- the first weekend of the month- at one of the monasteries in his name, and the second weekend at his convent in Old Cairo of which mother Kereya is the Abbess, to get her blessing. So, I had to double check if I was in the right place.

The nun was amazed and informed Tamav Kereya of his story, so she welcomed him and they prayed the mass together. After the mass, the priest revealed to the nuns that, "Something extraordinary will happen towards the end of this month, something I can't speak of right now, but you will know later!"

By that he meant Tamav's departure to heaven, and how St George didn't want him to miss out on her blessings and so he invited him to the convent. That was just one month before she passed away.

BEFORE HER DEPARTURE

As is the case all the time with righteous people who try to excel in virtue and grace, Satan never ceases to test them with tribulations and adversities. He increased her trials, moving bad people against her with evil to distress her, till she was literally suffocating. Nuns used to hear her, standing in front of the icon of St George, pleading in tears for his intercession to God to take her away from this world and rest her soul as soon as possible as it was much more than she could handle. She was very healthy around that time.

HER DEPARTURE

A few days later, on the 10th of August 1980, she felt a little sick with a slight fever, and then she got better a short while later. She wanted to attend the mass in the morning, so one of the nuns offered to accompany her to church, as she feared for her lest she fell along the way. But she insisted on going alone.

When she got to church, early in the morning, she saw a body wrapped in a white linen shroud and placed at the bottom of the altar. She was surprised and started to wonder in herself "Who would that be?" Then she heard a voice saying, "This is you." She was surprised all the more and asked "How could that be, if I am still alive?" The voice answered, "This is where you will be after two days." She was stunned, but comforted.

She went out to find another nun waiting. The nun noticed the change on Tamav's face and thought it was due to the fever, but Tamav denied and informed her of the vision and of the news of her approaching departure and requested from her not to tell anyone else. Then she went to get some rest.

Shortly afterwards, the rest of the nuns came to check up on her as they were very worried. But she reassured them saying, "You know my daughters, after all paradise is such a very beautiful place." That was after she saw the vision.

Then on the same night, she went into a coma due to the high fever. The next morning all the nuns gathered around her with a great deal of people who felt the need to be there on that specific day without any previous bookings. They tried to lower the fever with strips of cloth soaked in cold water and antibiotic injections, but all to no avail. Miraculously she was calling for St George while she was in a coma.

When the late Mother Martha, from St Abu Sefein's convent, heard of the news of her sickness she hurried into the convent to tend to her, as the two were very close friends spiritually. Mother Martha stayed beside Tamav, fasting and praying incessantly to God to heal her. Then, Mother Martha went to the church to pray. While she was praying she saw a vision of three people standing in front of the middle altar shining brightly. As she drew closer, she saw St Mary, St Mina and Pope Kyrillos. They told her that it is done already, referring to God's will. She went out of the church comforted and asked for food to be brought for her to eat, and then she told all the nuns about the vision.

The nuns hurried and called the priests of the convent who prayed the absolution on her. Upon the end of the prayer, she gave her soul up to the heavens. That was at 10:00 pm, on Tuesday, 12th of August 1980. Upon her departure, a very strong smell of incense was released and filled the room.

AFTER HER BURIAL

After her burial, the wife of the man responsible for the burial came to the convent and told the people about a very strange phenomenon that she and her husband noticed. Every Sunday, a strong smell of incense used to be emitted from the place where Tamav was buried. The nuns came to the cemetery to check the phenomenon, and they found it to be true, so they glorified God who honours his saints in such a way. That phenomenon continued for many years after her burial.

Another lady by the name of Mrs Linda Shafeek Shehata tells that she used to resort to Tamav for help with her financial issues. One day, as the demands of her family became more than she could afford, she felt so helpless and started crying about the hardship and bills she had to pay with no money on the table. She fell asleep and dreamt that night that Tamav had visited her, touched her face with the cross and asked her to stop crying, and to go to the convent as she was accustomed to and that the nuns there will help to solve her debts and will give her even more than before. She woke up comforted, with a very overwhelming feeling of peace and certainty that everything would be alright.

She did as she was told and went to the convent and got all the help she needed. This incident goes to show that Tamav Kereya never lost touch with her loved ones and those ones in need after she departed from our mortal world and indeed that she is always there to help whoever calls upon her.

REMARKS OF TAMAV ERINI

My relationship with Mother Kereya began before I entered the convent, as we were communicating by letters, while she was a nun in St Abu Sefein's convent.

She had a pure and merciful heart, to the extent that she used to distribute all her belongings to the needy, and as if that was not enough, she used to secretly visit the needy families and provide for their needs without anyone knowing.

Her life as a nun was a perfect example to all. She used to work all day and pray all night, and she always ran away from evildoers.

Her departure saddened me extremely and affected my blood pressure, so that even the doctors could not lower it by any means. However, I asked our Lord to comfort me, so Pope Kyrillos appeared and prayed for me. I asked him about mother Kereya, he answered and said, "She is in a beautiful place, she did not dream of it, but she deserved it because of her merciful work." Soon after I woke up from my sleep, my blood pressure became normal, so we prayed a mass in her memory. During the mass I saw her so I asked her if she was happy, she answered, "Very happy and I did not expect such a beautiful place." I also asked her what work had helped her to achieve this, she said, "Love and mercy."

Miraculously, the reading on the day of her burial (7 Misra) was a summary of Mother Kereya's life. Psalms 102:19-21; Mark 12:41-44; Romans 1:1-17; Acts 7:2-7

Her prayers and blessing be with us all Amen

www.ingramcontent.com/pod-product-compliance
Lightning Source LLC
Chambersburg PA
CBHW021914040426
42447CB00007B/857